MW01181724

Color
Me
SMART

The Busy Business Owner's Guide
to Seeing Your Company in Color

Vickie Musni

ISBN- 13: 978-0-692-10659-4

Author Photo by Edyta Sokolowska, Owner, Exceed Photography LLC

To bring Vickie to your location to speak to your group or organization call 775-772-9188 or go to www.VickieMusni.com

Printed in the United States of America

First Edition

CONTENTS

SECTION 5 – RELATIONSHIPS

SECTION 6 – TEAMS

SECTION 7

SECTION 1

CHAPTER 1

Seeing in Color

Imagine you are a fly on the wall at a party. What personalities might you see? The loud ones, telling their jokes and stories with a laughter you hear from across the room. The quiet ones, feeling a little lost, seeking out a quiet corner or someone else who might find comfort in sipping a drink in silence while deep in thought. You notice the "take charge" ones who are always busy…hanging up someone's coat, refilling the punch bowl, and putting fresh towels out on the bathroom counter. Then you see the ones who can blend in and mingle with different groups and make small talk for a while, but who eventually find someone they know or like to spend the remainder of the party with.

Does this scene seem familiar? These different types of interactions are happening at office parties, school parties, or other social events all over. Different people have different personalities…and for centuries, people have been trying to understand each other and all of those diverse personalities.

The first known studies of personality types dates back to approximately 400 B.C. Hippocrates was the first one to categorize people based on four "temperaments" that he observed. Almost any four "quadrant" system that you may have heard about, read about, or taken a test for, probably traces its roots back to this great thinker in Ancient Greece. We are still talking about these personality differences thousands of years later because there is still so much truth in them!

Over the years, many people have added their own thoughts, observations and research, but I think what really helps separate one "system" from another is the *way* in which the concepts are explained, remembered, and applied. I did not "invent" the four personality types that I teach but when you read my books, you get my perspective…and from my perspective, using four colors is the most effective way I have found to explain this information in a way that can easily be remembered and applied.

Maybe it's my Red side, but I want you to be able to understand the different personalities quickly, remember them easily, and be able to apply what you are learning immediately to real life situations and relationships. In short, I want you to be able to see everyone in your business, and in your life, *in color*.

Most of us go through life without truly noticing so much of what is happening around us. We can see, but we don't observe. We must train ourselves to look deeply at situations and people, to examine personality differences, and strive to understand what might be going on beneath the surface. As much as I love a good personality test (and the *Wired that Way Assessment* is definitely my favorite!) there are just too many situations where it simply isn't practical to ask someone to take a test. Can you imagine asking a customer who walks into your store or office to take a 40-question test before they shop so you can know their personality before you try to sell to them? Definitely NOT a technique I recommend.

Instead, imagine yourself being completely present, focused on the new customer before you. What do you notice about the way she is dressed? You notice his posture. You focus on the words she uses. You pay attention to his volume and tone. What if you could take all of these clues, "see" them through the lens of personalities, and recognize what matters most to them early on in the conversation? Could you connect with new clients more deeply? Could you solve their problems faster? Could you provide a better, more personalized experience for them? Imagine the impact this could have on your business.

This, my friend, is what I refer to as *seeing in color.*

Personal Reflection or Group Discussion

1. How would you describe the personalities of each person on your team?
2. To what extent do you think personalities affect your business?
3. Do you see personalities affecting your business more internally (how team members relate with one another) or externally (how you interact with others like clients or vendors)?

To Go Deeper - Order a copy of the Wired That Way Assessment Tool for each member of your team. (Amazon.com)

CHAPTER 2

Your Guide to Colors

With a quick look around your office, school or home, you can tell that there are as many different types of people as there are colors. Let's start identifying specific, noticeable traits and begin painting a picture of the different personality colors. If you are already familiar with the three most common identifiers for each personality as I teach them, feel free to skip to the last paragraph of this chapter.

There are four primary personality colors. (Yes, I realize there are only three primary colors, but color is really just an analogy to help us remember the personality types and give us a common vocabulary to describe what we observe and know. So just hang with me on the whole four colors thing.) Yellow, Blue, Red and Green. Picture them as a chart with four quadrants. They are all wonderful...and beautiful...and special...and equally needed, cherished, and valued. However, I simply cannot explain all four of them at the same time.

Yellow	Red
Green	Blue

Yellows  Jimmy Katie Zoe Jaxx

I have to start somewhere, so I begin with Yellow. This is not because Yellow is the best personality type, or the most important. It is simply because Yellows are the easiest to identify. Yellows are LOUD…loud in voice, and often in dress. You can spot a Yellow coming, and often you can hear them before you can even see them. You know those people who tell their stories really loud because they love having an audience? The ones who love bright colors, bold prints, and all things that shine and sparkle? Yellows.

Yellows are also noticeable because they tend to be very OPEN. Life is an open book, and their mouths are usually open. They share openly and are often guilty of sharing TMI…too much information. Do you have people in your life who always seem to be "in trouble" or are always getting "shushed"? The ones who tend to share too much too soon or too often, or too loudly? Do you know people who can strike up a conversation with anyone? The ones who make friends in line at the grocery store and on airplanes because they speak so openly to everyone around them? Yellows.

The third most observable indicator of a Yellow is CLUTTER. Yellows tend to be on the messy side. Their desks are often covered in piles because filing something "away" is dangerous for Yellows… out of sight, out of mind. You might notice a trail with Yellows…. wrappers and receipts, telling of the stories of where they've been, and what they've been snacking on. Do you see a messy car? A huge purse with "everything" in it? Usually, this means Yellow.

Loud, open, and cluttered. Is this you? Or someone you know? When you think of these traits, begin to associate them with the color yellow…think bright and sunny and you won't forget these easy to spot personalities.

Blues

The personality type opposite of Yellow is Blue. As you might guess, the Blue indicators are also fairly easy to identify because they are the opposite of the Yellow indicators. The first one is *quiet*. Blues tend to speak more quietly, dress more quietly, and carry themselves more quietly. They often choose more muted or neutral colors to wear, because they tend to prefer blending in rather than wearing something that will attract a lot of attention. Blues tend to prefer a quiet working environment that will be conducive to analyzing details and pondering deep thoughts.

Blues also tend to be more *closed*. While Yellows tend to say whatever pops into their head to whoever happens to be around, Blues tend to be more private. They need to know someone longer before they begin sharing personal information. Generally speaking, Blues have a smaller number of close friends, oftentimes people they have known for many years. Blues have what I describe as a privacy bubble. Not only do they have a more defined sense of personal space, they are very selective about who they let inside.

I'm sure you've heard the old adage "a place for everything and everything in its place." That phrase was created by Blues, and is embraced by Blues everywhere. Yes, *neat and tidy* is the third Blue indicator. Both things and ideas need to be stored in an orderly fashion which means organizers, label makers, and file folders are usually as loved and appreciated by Blues as graphs, charts and spreadsheets.

Quiet, closed and organized. Is this you? Someone you work with or for? Or perhaps you are like our family and Blue seems to be missing completely. Either way, associate these deep traits with Blue like the ocean and you will soon be able to understand these Blue qualities whether they describe you or not.

Reds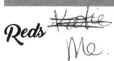

The next easiest-to-spot personality color is Red. The first thing most people notice about Reds is their ENERGY. Reds have an unmistakable energy about them, a "presence" that is felt as soon as they enter a room. Reds are busy, always on the go, and generally keep a full calendar and are moving at a fast pace.

A visible trait shared by many Reds is bold, distinct HAND GESTURES. A Red's natural gestures often include things that other personalities tend to interpret as negative like finger-pointing, hands on hips, fist pounding, or crossed arms. Do not be fooled; these gestures do not always mean that the Red individual is angry or upset. Sometimes this is just the way they are. An action like placing hands on hips is often what I'll call the Red "default thinking position."

Another common trait is that they tend to be very PRACTICAL. Reds have a built-in need for efficiency. They will usually make the most logical choice, which often means the most versatile clothing and classic and/or comfortable footwear. They are good at quickly assessing a situation and knowing the most efficient way to reach the desired goal.

High energy, bold hand gestures, and very practical. Does this sound like you? Or does this remind you of someone you know? There should be no questioning why we use the color red to identify this fiery personality.

Greens

There is a reason why we discuss Green traits last. Do you know why? We started with the personality colors most easy to identify and Greens are most often the hardest to recognize. Yellows are spotted because they are extremely loud and "everywhere" and Blues for the extreme quiet and orderly appearance and behavior. Reds are extremely high energy and active, yet Greens are not "extremely" anything. *Process of elimination* is most often the first identifier of a Green. Greens possess a unique chameleon-like ability to take on the traits of the other colors, at least for a while, depending on the situation they are in. Their lack of "extremeness" makes them very adaptable and they can get along with most people, most of the time.

Greens are naturally very *cool, calm and collected.* They tend to not overreact to things and are really comforting to have around in times of emergencies. Hopefully in a real emergency you will have at least one Red with you so someone is there to call a tow truck or 9-1-1 or make a quick decision about what needs to be done, but having a Green friend with you can just make you feel better by their peaceful presence.

Not only are Greens good at comforting others, but they also tend to place a high value on personal comfort, or can find a way to become comfortable. *Comfort* is the third identifier to look for with Greens. Often Greens are the most casually dressed for what a given situation would allow, and are usually the first ones to sit down, recline, or put their feet up.

If process of elimination and observation lead you to the comfort of one who is cool, calm, and collected, chances are good you are looking at a Green. Visualize peaceful green meadows as your association for this personality.

Now that we've established some of the most common identifiers of each personality color, I want to be quick to add that you must allow for differences. Please don't try to paint people with too broad of a brush. Keep in mind that there are many shades and hues of each color and the same is true for personalities. If you look around where you are sitting right now, I bet you can spot several different shades of blue. Even though the blue of your jeans doesn't match the blue of the sky, your brain still recognizes them as blue. Please keep this in mind as we move forward and begin to explore various areas of business and life where we need to see people in color.

Personal Reflection or Group Discussion

1. Do you see any of these traits in yourself?
2. Which of these traits do you observe in others on your team?
3. Begin to think about clients or vendors you interact with regularly. What colors can you see in some of those people?

To Go Deeper - Take time to complete the Wired that Way assessment that was recommended at the end of Chapter One. Are the answers in line with your initial observations?

Sales

CHAPTER 3

Different Colored Shoppers

As a Certified Personality Trainer, I speak at a lot of conferences and events as well as offering company training and private coaching. I help people understand personality types and apply that knowledge to life and business. Can you guess the number one topic I get asked to speak about the most? Yes, sales. This book is going to cover all the areas from the Color Me SMART program – Sales, Marketing, Abilities, Relationships and Teams. But we'll start with sales because this seems to be what every business owner and sales manager is thinking about. (And let's be honest, SMART starts with "S" so *Sales* has to come first.)

If you have read my first book, *Personalities for Business*, you may remember that I began the section on sales with personal stories to illustrate some of the differences in the way different personalities shop. As a Yellow, I impulsively bought a red convertible from Craigslist because all I wanted was a fun car. I talked about buying appliances with my Blue engineer father who had to read every detail and every review and report before making a decision. (And how once again I just wanted the red washer and dryer because it would make having to do laundry more fun). As a Red, I shared about having to go to three different carpet places because the first salespeople weren't willing/able to sell me what I wanted and I was upset by them wasting my time and trying to change my mind. And then there was the story of my Green husband who would rather I just text him a picture with two options so he wouldn't even have to go to the store. Can you relate? Not everyone shops the same way.

Let's look at another common buying situation, online shopping, and how each different personality approaches it. Online shopping is a great example of an "everyday situation" and how each personality type has the ability to look at the exact same situation from a different perspective. What I have noticed about online shopping is that different personalities tend to like it for different reasons. Understanding the *motivation* behind why a person chooses to shop online, and how they make their online buying decisions, is what we will look at briefly now.

Please keep in mind that these are *generalizations*. They are not true for 100% of the people, AND many people fit into more than one category (usually having a primary and a secondary color). That being said, as with most generalizations, these observations are true much of the time. Let's look at how the different colors may approach online shopping:

- Yellows love fun, excitement, and attention. So in general, they are the ones who enjoy the "adventure" of going shopping, and go with friends whenever possible. The biggest reason that Yellows like to buy online? They get the "buyer's high" from shopping TWICE....once when they hit send, and once when the package arrives! What is more fun than getting a package in the mail?!
- Blues are the deep thinking, analytical type. Being able to compare features, benefits, prices, reviews, ratings, guarantees and more, with limited if any social interaction...online shopping is PERFECT for Blues!
- A true Red values efficiency in any decision making process. To be able to order things "immediately" without having to

drive to a store, look up and down different aisles, and waste time waiting in line…again, the perfect option.

- Greens are motivated by their need for peace and comfort. What could be more comfortable than being able to purchase what you need while lying on the couch in your pajamas?

The *action* in this example – buying something online – is essentially the same. The thing that is different for each personality is the *motivation* and the *thought process* behind the action. That is the part we need to try to understand both about ourselves, and about others who may be different from us.

Now, take this idea of motivation and thought process into your own business and begin to examine your own sales situations. How do you "usually" sell to potential client? Do you have a standard pitch that you use? Do you have certain lines that you try to say to everyone… because they've worked well in the past and you think they will again? Stop.

Stop thinking that you can find one magic formula that will "work" on any person. Start being SMART. Start seeing in color. What personality color does that individual who sits before you seem to be? What do you think is her primary motivation? Is it fun? Is it order or perfection? Is it efficiency? Is it simplicity and comfort? Start by trying to create the right atmosphere. Continue by trying to get to the core of what he needs and wants. Ask questions that will help you confirm your hypothesis about her personality preference as you move farther into the sales process. Each shopper is unique. Start acting that way.

Personal Reflection or Group Discussion

1. How do you like to shop?

2. Have you ever gone shopping with someone whose "shopping style" was different from yours? What was that experience like for you?

3. What kind of shopping experiences are you providing for the clients who buy from you?

To Go Deeper - Brainstorm ways that you can create colorful ways for different personalities to buy from you in a way that meets their unique needs and preferences. What options can you provide that allow for personality differences?

CHAPTER 4

Looking for Clues Face to Face and Online

If each shopper is unique and will benefit by being treated according to his or her unique personality color, how do you determine the color of the client? I joked in Chapter 1 about the absurdity of asking a customer to take a personality test. If you can't get them to take a test and identify their personality type, how do you know which type(s) of people you are trying to sell to? YOU have to figure it out. Put on your figurative detective hat and start looking for color clues.

Is your first point of contact with a potential client usually in person? Perhaps the first time you see him is when he walks into your store, studio, office, or other meeting space. Or maybe she finds you at some type of industry trade show when she walks up to your booth. No matter the situation where you first see them, you must train yourself to start seeing people in color from the time that you meet them.

Think about the descriptions in Chapter 2 about the most common identifiers of each color. What do you see – and hear – that will give you clues?

How loud are they?
What color and style clothing are they wearing?

Do they seem scattered? (Think about actual or "mental" clutter.)
How do they carry themselves? Quiet? Confident? Cautious? Friendly?
What types of hand gestures do they use?
What kind of tone do you sense when they speak? Fun and upbeat? Thoughtful and serious? Straight to the point? Relaxed? Or maybe, overwhelmed or indecisive?

Remember: the goal of identifying personality types is to help you *understand* the other person so that you can *solve* their problems. This material is not intended to be used to encourage stereotypes or to enable you to manipulate people. The goal of sales is to solve a problem, and understanding the potential client through the lens of personalities can help you understand them better, connect sooner, and get to the heart of what they really need earlier in the process.

Next, really listen to the words they use. Look for "buzz words" in their speech that could be indicators not only of personality type, but of their priorities and motivation. The following list is by no means exhaustive but will help you start listening to your clients in color.

Yellow: fun, exciting, shine/shiny, stand out, colorful, new, unique, attention, stories, bright, surprise, loud, engaging	Red: efficient, practical, impressive, quick, fast, win, best, I/me/my, concise, guarantee, competition
Green: peaceful, comfortable, relaxed, friendly, overwhelming, need help, calm, chill, harmony, understanding, warm, inviting	Blue: perfect, orderly, organized, plan(ned), research, data, precise, neat, system, files, labels, quiet, as expected

It is usually easier to identify personalities when you meet in person, but what about all those situations where that isn't the case? What if your first point of contact is over the phone, text, social media message, email or an online inquiry form? The answer is still *look for clues.* You may not be able to see what they are wearing, but you can still get a sense from their word choice, length of message or overall tone. If over the phone, most of the first list of questions still apply. How loud are they? How fast or slow do they speak? What is their tone? And whether you are having a conversation in person, over the phone, or in some form of written text, their words will still contain valuable clues. Look for them.

Depending on your business and what you sell, this next part may or may not apply to you. If you have a store or restaurant and your customers are coming to you, focus on the hints above. But if you get email inquiries or social media messages as the first point of contact, I encourage you to go one step farther and do a little extra searching for clues *before* you even reply.

I love to pop a name or email into Facebook and see what comes up. You can find LOTS of personality clues by looking at someone's profile photo, cover image and any public posts. I have done this for years, but I admit that I used to feel a little awkward about it…until Mitch Taylor, fellow author, speaker and sales trainer, put things into perspective for me: *Your prospective clients are googling you, why aren't you googling them?*

Remember, this tip is to help you learn a little more about a person so you can make an educated guess as to their personality type and decide the best, most effective way to reply to an individual inquiry. You don't need to go overboard or be creepy about it. Just look to see if they have a public profile. This may help you discern how "open" they are. Do they have a lot of selfies or photos with large groups of friends? Or do you see "less" – perhaps just that person or one or two other people in their featured photos?

Looking for clues is an important part of being SMART in your sales process. Pay attention to the words that are used in speech or in text. Look for any other color indicators that you can see, hear, or find, and make your best guess. In the next chapter we'll look at how to use the things you've noticed to help you not only *see* in color but begin to *speak* in color.

Personal Reflection or Group Discussion

1. Think about the last client you met in person? What color do you think he or she is?
2. Look at the last online inquiry that you received. What clues can you find that will help you make an educated guess as to that person's color?

To Go Deeper - Guessing client colors is fun, but it's more important that you find a way to use the information that you discover. What systems can you implement to help you remember the color of regular clients? How can you use this information to provide a better personalized experience for each of them?

CHAPTER 5

Finding Words that Meet Needs

At the core of each personality type is a primary need...something inbuilt that provides the primary motivation for decisions. Selling, at its core, is about meeting needs...solving problems. To do that well you must really understand not only what a person wants, (and it doesn't matter if we're talking toothpaste or a dream wedding) but what his or her personality *needs* and how that affects the decision making process. Let's take a closer look at those examples.

Hopefully everyone uses toothpaste. But how different people decide which toothpaste to buy can vary greatly.

- Yellows will likely go with whatever option tastes the best and will spare them any socially awkward moments that could result from having bad breath.
- A Blue is more likely to research different options, see what the dentist recommends, or compare the cost per ounce for any scientifically, legitimately recommended brands.
- Reds will tend to grab whatever brand name they recognize that they spot first, as long as it is on sale.

- A Green might just use his roommate's toothpaste until he has a chance to go to the store, and then he will just get the same kind he has always used.

Why? Yellows have an innate need for attention and acceptance. Blues have wired within them a need for perfection and will go to great lengths to make the "right" decision. Reds need efficiency as much as Greens need comfort and simplicity. So, if you were trying to sell toothpaste to these four different people, would you say the same thing to each one of them? If you know you've got a Yellow in front of you, and you know that most Yellows are hyper-aware of social situations, what people think of them, and they always have their mouths open...why not start with how great this brand is at getting rid of bad breath and keeping your mouth feeling fresh longer? If you have a Blue, go ahead and start with the details of all the cavity-fighting and plaque-preventing properties. Reds? Show that it is a good value using as few words as possible. Green? Here's a two-pack so you won't have to worry about buying more for months!

Finding the right words that demonstrate that you understand how a person feels and what they need is important. If thinking this way can help create customers of small things, like toothpaste, imagine the impact that seeing and speaking in color can have on people and companies who sell bigger items or provide services. I expect that you know a LOT about what you sell. (I certainly hope so.) You could probably share a lot of features and benefits about your products or services, and I bet you have lots of stories from satisfied customers. Be SMART about using the personality clues that you've gathered and use that information to help you decide where to take that conversation. Let color clues show you what you should lead with and what you should leave out.

For the wedding example...can you make a Yellow bride feel like a princess? Show her how. Let her experience what it is like to have the full princess experience from the moment you meet. Can you ease the fears of a Blue who has the perfect wedding planned in her head and wants to know if you can deliver that? Walk through her detailed list of needs and concerns, one by one, with the level of detail that she needs to trust you. Want to earn the wedding business of a Red? Show her that you value her time by being on time, not over-explaining or over-selling, and only answering the questions she asks. If Reds feels respected by you, they are more likely to want to work with you. Can you take away the stress of a Green bride? Simplify options, provide fewer choices, and do everything you can to make it easy on her. Make it easy to work with you.

When you can identify the inner need of an individual and focus your attention on meeting that need, sales will come. Seeing in color helps you get to a deeper place of connection, sooner. I've given you two examples here. Take some time now to examine what you sell from a color personality perspective. How would each color view your product or service? How can you find the "one thing" that is most likely to resonate with each type? What is that makes it fun? How can you bring order or perfection to a situation? Can you add value by increasing efficiency? Can you make a situation more comfortable or a problem more peaceful?

Personal Reflection or Group Discussion

1. Identify the "one thing" for each color. What is it about your product or service that will most directly "speak" to each color?
2. Write down your answers to the above question for each personality.
3. How can you begin to work those ideas into your sales conversations in a way that is both natural to you and helpful to the client?

To Go Deeper - Role play some common sales situations with your team. How should you answer questions from each personality type.

BONUS – THE SALES PROCESS

Adapted from the book *SALES 4 Event Pros* by Mitch Taylor

Search – Before you reply to an online inquiry, return a phone call or set a meeting with the prospect, SEARCH for clues about them using the information they give you. Look for color clues in the language they use and the photos or posts you can see with a quick social media search.

Approach – Use what you learned in your Search to put yourself in the right mindset. Do you need to be energized? Relaxed? Quiet and reserved? Focused and direct? Mentally prepare the best you can and then adjust your tone and words as needed at the meeting. Begin with Mitch Taylor's two key questions: (1) How did you hear about us? (2) What do you know about us as a company?

Learn – Ask GREAT questions. Make sure your questions are:

- Open-ended (Focus on *How* or *Why*...not "yes or no" questions.)
- Conversational (Be yourself and don't read from a list!)
- Emotional (Buying decisions are made on emotion, then justified on logic.)

Then, LISTEN. Don't interrupt, and don't talk too much.

Explain – Showcase your expertise in a way that is helpful, keeping the emphasis on the client's needs and not how great you, your product or service is. Explain how you have solved a similar problem in the past and brainstorm ways you can be a part of their solution.

Solve – Don't focus on a "closing" a deal. Focus on how you can SOLVE the problem or issue that this client is facing. Show social proof from past clients in the form of reviews, testimonials, videos or surveys. Present options, and ask for the sale. Be friendly and helpful through the end of the conversation, and always end with a plan to follow up...whether or not a transaction occurs at that meeting.

For more information about SALES 4 Event Pros and other products and services from Mitch Taylor, visit www.TayloredSales.com.

For a full color downloadable PDF of this Bonus page please go to www.VickieMusni.com/SMARTbonuses.

Marketing

S
A
R
T

CHAPTER 6

What color is your audience?

The M in SMART is for Marketing. The first question in Marketing 101...who are you trying to reach? "Customers" or "people who will buy from me" are not really the kind of answers we are looking for when it comes to identifying a target audience for your marketing. I want you to describe them...in detail...*in color*.

Many times, we get so focused on looking forward – *who do I need to reach next?* – that we forget the importance of looking backward. Think back over the last year, or even longer. Who did you LOVE working with? Which clients allowed you to do your BEST work? Which patients or students made you look FORWARD to going to work each day? Which customers made you SMILE and reminded you WHY you do what you do?

Make a list. Write out their names. Look at pictures or client files if you have them. Now ask yourself, what exactly was it about these people that made me feel this way? Are there traits that these past clients have in common? What are they? *Write them down.* In addition to answering questions about age, gender, profession, income/education level, interests and other "general marketing" data, I want you to take a long hard look at your list of favorite customers *in color*.

Even if you are new to thinking about people in terms of personality colors, look at your list and try to identify the colors of the people on your list. What patterns do you see? Do you love the fun, creativity, and excitement of working with Yellows? Or does their flakiness or tardiness stress you out? Do you love poring over details and plotting data on spreadsheets with your Blue clients, or does that love of detail – and quiet! – make you cringe? Do you enjoy working with Reds who know exactly what they want? Do Reds with a narrow focus make your job easier, or do you find yourself butting heads with them or feeling underappreciated? Do you love coming alongside Greens and helping them find peaceful solutions to their problems through your services? Or does their indecisiveness or slower pace make you feel less excited or fulfilled?

It is okay to have a "favorite" personality color when it comes to your clients. However, it may or may not be realistic or wise for you to focus your marketing efforts to "speak" to that one type of client. Sometimes we don't get to choose who we work with. Or sometimes "the client" is really more than one person. For example, if you teach private lessons or do private tutoring you may have a child with one personality, and a parent who is a different color. I have worked in the wedding industry for over two decades, both working with couples and coaching or training other wedding professionals. I can say this, I have never heard of a wedding with only one client. While it may be true in many cases that the bride has the final "say" in the matter, there are ALWAYS at least two clients for weddings (and often more if you are dealing with multiple parents involved, really "helpful" maids of honor, etc.). And it is very common to have a couple that are a good example of "opposites attracting" so even if you do have an ideal personality color in mind for your perfect clients, it will always be advantageous for you if you can "speak" to all of the colors. This was true in the Sales section, and it is equally true with marketing.

It is important to identify the personalities of the clients you most want to reach with your marketing pieces. But you should also keep in mind how other personality colors may interpret what they see about you and your company. In the next chapter we will look at some ideas to make sure you have "something" for every color.

Personal Reflection or Group Discussion

1. Who are your "favorite" clients from the past 12 months?
2. What are the traits that made you love working with them?
3. What patterns do you see? Are there one or two colors that you love working with most?

To Go Deeper - Discuss "favorite clients" with your team. Are your lists of favorite clients similar or different? Can you identify patterns of colors of team members who work really well (or not-so-well) with certain colors of clients? Brainstorm ways that you can match clients and team members in the best way possible. What ideas do you have for trying to find more clients with the traits that your team loves?

CHAPTER 7

What Color is Your Marketing?

It is basic human nature for us to speak according to our personality type. Unless trained to do otherwise, people will generally speak in a way that they like to be spoken to. We do it in person. We do it when we write texts or emails. And we do it with other forms of communication…often including marketing pieces that we create. In Chapter 4 we took a look at how color personalities play into sales conversations; the same concepts apply to marketing.

Let's start with a simple exercise. Take out your business card and look at it from a color personality perspective. What "color" is your card? Keep in mind of course that this often has nothing to do with the colors printed on the card. A "Yellow" personality card may be bright fuchsia and a "Red" personality card could be all black and white.

What overall look and feel does it have? Consider color combinations, font size, wording, graphics and even size, texture, weight and shape. Does it seem to "speak" one language, or maybe two, more so than the other colors? Would you describe it as exciting and fun? Thoughtful and serious? Bold and energetic? Warm and friendly? Does your card reflect your personality? Does it "speak" to the personality of your ideal client? Or maybe both?

There is no right or wrong answer for this exercise. Every business model is different, and even among the four personality types, people are still different and can have different likes, dislikes, or styles. But examining something as simple as a business card can help you begin to see marketing in color.

Consider now other marketing that you do. Do you have printed materials such as brochures, posters, invitations or catalogues? What about your social media presences? What are the personality colors in the tone of your posts? With your choice of images? In the words that you choose? Compare your observations with your conclusions from the previous business card exercise.

Does your marketing seem to have a primary personality color, or a blend of two? How does this compare to your personal personality color? And perhaps more importantly, how do your observations about your marketing and social media presence compare to your assessment of your company's personality color? Social media trends are changing constantly so I am not going to go into great detail about what this could look like within a particular platform, but what I really want you to take from this section is a reminder to be SMART in how you approach social media. Look at your profiles, posts and interactions with others in *color.*

Even with changing social media marketing trends, and the ability to adapt words on posters or print new business cards with relative ease, you likely have another important marketing tool: your website. Hopefully you will have overlapping design elements across your print, social and website. Websites are a powerful tool in your marketing toolbox, as most search engine queries and even social media platforms can lead a client there. But once they are there, you must connect right away. In the next chapter we'll take a deeper look at an example of a site that speaks all four colors really well.

Personal Reflection or Group Discussion

1. What observations can you make about your business card in terms of personality color?
2. Does your card have a primary and/or secondary personality?
3. Are the personality colors of your card in alignment with the personality color you want your company to reach?

To Go Deeper - Ask three other trusted colleagues to describe your card. Ideally, look for people who are different personality colors. If those people "speak" in color, great. If not, you may have to "translate" their remarks. It is important to ask others what they see as others often see things differently. What "colors" are they seeing?

CHAPTER 8

Colorful Websites

A company can have a personality, and that can certainly be reflected in a website. But if you came to the conclusion in Chapter 6 that your clients span all four color categories, you need to make sure that your website has something for every color. You need to connect quickly with each visitor, so being aware of all four colors and how they "see" your home or landing page is really important.

One of the best examples I have seen of a website that reflects the company's personality and "speaks" to all four colors, is the one for my dentist office, Aland Family Dentistry in Reno, Nevada. Because I have done company training for their staff, I know there are quite a few Greens there. There is also a strong Yellow presence there...there are postcards on the ceiling, games in the lobby (tic tac toe for grown-ups!) and photo books of their latest staff trip to Disneyland. They are a FUN group, and really good at making people feel COMFORTABLE.

When you first land at www.AlandFamilyDentistry.com, you will see a rotating collage of friendly, smiling faces of individuals, pairs and groups. The pace of the rotation is fairly slow, showcasing both softer smiles as well as big laughs. All of that subtly speaks the language of Yellows and Greens. The text to the right of the photos reads,

"Having a beautiful, healthy smile brings you confidence and happiness. We are dedicated to helping you achieve the smile of your dreams with an exceptional dental experience. Let us help YOU have a winning smile!" I love this example because those three short sentences have multiple "buzz words" for each personality color. The whole thing is positive and written with an audience focus, but there are certain words that are more likely to resonate strongly with certain colors. Here is my assessment of the above text:

Yellow Words: beautiful, dreams, exceptional	Red Words: confidence, achieve, winning
Green Words: happiness, Let us Help YOU	Blue Words: healthy, dedicated, experience

The next sentence in the spot below says, "At Aland Family Dentistry, we provide compassionate and gentle dental care to our patients from throughout Northern Nevada. <u>Dr. Troy E. Aland</u> and our highly-skilled dental <u>team</u> believe our patients are our friends, and as such, deserve to be treated with warmth, respect, and consideration. Dr. Aland and our team always make the effort to ensure that every visit to our practice is a positive one for patients and their families." Here is my list for that section:

Yellow Words: friends, positive, families	Red Words: respect, always, effort, ensure
Green Words: compassionate, gentle, warmth	Blue Words: highly–skilled, consideration, Dr. Troy E. Aland and "team" have links to more details

Do you see why I love this site so much as an example of marketing to different color personalities? This site does a great job of reflecting the company's primary colors (Yellow and Green) while using verbiage and imagery that will resonate with each color. I challenge you to take a look at your own website using the *What Color is Your Website?* Color Analysis Chart.

Personal Reflection or Group Discussion

1. Look at the homepage of your website. What personality color(s) do you see most?
2. Are the words and images the same colors as the clients you decided you most want to reach?
3. If you have decided that your clients are indeed all four colors, does your website have "something" for each one?

To Go Deeper - Use the *What Color is Your Website?* Color Analysis Chart from the bonus material to do a thorough analysis of your website. Enlist your team for help with this and pay special attention to their thoughts, ideas, and observations that might be different from your own.

BONUS – WHAT COLOR IS YOUR WEBSITE? COLOR ANALYSIS CHART

Use the following chart to assess the color(s) of your website. Line by line (even if you are a Yellow!) examine each facet of the page and identify elements that "speak" to each personality color. Do this separately for each page of your website noting impressions, common themes, and specific words.

	Yellow	Blue	Red	Green
Overall impression				
Color scheme				
Shapes/Lines				
Images				
Menu Bar/ Navigation				
Primary Text				
Secondary Text				
Interactive Elements (links, videos, etc.)				
Other Observations				

For a full color downloadable PDF of this Bonus page please go to www.VickieMusni.com/SMARTbonuses.

S
M
R
T

Abilities

CHAPTER 9

Embracing Your Color Strengths

The A in SMART is for ABILITIES. Every personality comes with its own set of *natural* abilities. Yes, many people also possess "learned skills," but natural abilities play a huge part in how you operate your business, lead your team, and perform tasks.

Every color personality has a propensity toward different strengths and weaknesses. Remember that in much the same way there are different shades of each color, there are also different "shades" of personality colors. Not everyone will share every single strength or every single weaknesses. However, there are many common traits for each type. For you to truly be your best self, and have the best interactions with others, you must take an honest assessment of your own personality. We're going to start with strengths because that is always more fun to think about. Learning not only to identify the positive characteristics that come naturally to you, but also to leverage them to create the best situations and possible relationships is really what this chapter is about.

When I am doing a team training or interactive workshop, one of my favorite activities is to divide everyone into personality groups and ask them to make a list of their strengths and weaknesses, usually beginning with the strengths. Yellows seem to love this assignment. Yellows are naturally positive so it is usually easy for them to list all of their positive traits. Besides positivity, other common answers include being able to strike up a conversation with anyone, being the life of the party, having a contagious enthusiasm, creativity, and being spontaneous and fun.

Blues tend to be a little slower building their list of strengths, but eventually they come up with a list...a very neatly written and sometimes alphabetized list. Identified strengths include things like being good at lists, charts, and graphs, understanding details, analytical, and organized. They are also loyal friends, good listeners, and conscientious workers. Some Blues struggle with this activity because their perfectionist nature can cause them to be very self-critical, but that quest for high achievement is definitely a strength.

The Red group is always quick to make a thorough list of their natural abilities. Occasionally there may be a bit of a power struggle over who will serve as the "scribe" for the group but their list is comprised of words such as natural-born leader, bold, dynamic, risk-taker, rises to the challenge, efficient, good at finding practical solutions quickly, great in emergencies, and usually right. (That last one will trigger some indignant laughter or eye rolls from the other groups.)

The Greens are usually the last group to finish and sometimes need a little prodding. Most of the time they come up with a great list of natural strengths like being easy to talk to, slow and steady, compassionate, peacemaker, patient, sympathetic, easy-going, and easy to get along with.

How about you? What else would you add to these lists of strengths? Which ones do you see as your greatest assets?

There are two main reasons I spend so much time teaching about strengths. The first one is that it is important to understand and appreciate our own unique abilities. So much negativity exists in the world. Go ahead and let yourself focus on what you do well. Embrace those traits. Focus on them. Look for ways to use those abilities to improve your life and the lives of others. How much control do you have over your job duties? Do everything you can to put yourself in a position where you can use your natural abilities. Not only are you more likely to experience success when your responsibilities are in line with your abilities, but you are more likely to enjoy your tasks increasing both productivity and satisfaction.

The second reason is to help us appreciate the natural abilities that other personalities have. It is easy to become frustrated at times with people who are different from us. Focusing on the strengths of other personalities is one way of helping us learn to appreciate that other people are not like us. More often than not, the strengths of the other personalities bring balance to our weaknesses.

Several years ago I took a contract managing the wedding photography department for a large hotel property. For months I couldn't figure out why some days I loved that job, and other days I was miserable. But then I realized I was so busy focusing on what color my clients were and how I could provide the best sales experience possible for them, I hadn't been thinking about my position in relationship to my own personality. As a Yellow/Red, I loved the days when I had back to back sales meetings. My days were fun, full of great conversations and meeting new people. My Yellow side was happy. When I had back to back sales appointments and could rise to the challenge to fit it all in, make my clients happy, while earning a fantastic commission, my Red side was also happy.

However, the other side of my job involved some lonely days in my office that I shared with no one. It was me, my computer, and a bunch of spreadsheets about dates, times, and details. As an extrovert, I was miserable. The part of my job that was utilizing my natural abilities of connecting with people, solving problems, and meeting goals for my team, let me feel energized and excited. But the other days, I felt depressed and regularly thought about quitting. Instead of quitting, I did something better. I found a way to hire an administrative assistant to do the parts of my job that I didn't like. She was primarily Green with some Blue, and she loved the predictability of filling out the forms and updating the spreadsheets. Once I wasn't spending all that extra energy on the part that was outside of my natural abilities, I was free to really enjoy the parts of the job for which I was well suited.

How are you using your abilities in your business? Are there any adjustments that you can make that will allow you to experience more joy and fulfillment? See yourself in color and look for ways to maximize the strengths of your personality.

Personal Reflection or Group Discussion

1. Which personality strengths do you most see in yourself?
2. Of all the different tasks that you do for your job, which ones do you really love?
3. How do these match up with your natural strengths? Are there small changes that you could make that would allow you to do even more of the things that you love?

To Go Deeper - Use your results from the WTW assessment to analyze your top strengths as well as the strengths of your teammates. Take some time to compliment the other members of your team for things you have observed lately that they are particularly good at. If you are using this as a group discussion tool, do this out loud together. If you are working through this book on your own, send a written note to your team sharing something that you admire about one (or more) of their strengths.

CHAPTER 10

Working on Weaknesses

No one likes to talk about weaknesses. In fact, I've had many people advise me not to use the word, "weaknesses," in my training. But whether you call them "challenges" or "blind spots" or just plain "weaknesses" the truth is that we all have them…no matter what we choose to call them. We all have things that we are not naturally good at, habits that we struggle with, or obstacles that keep us from creating the results or relationships that we want. If you are serious about getting the most out of this book and the personality color system I teach, you need to take a really honest look at yourself and the weaknesses that you may be prone to.

The Wired That Way assessment tool measures the twenty most common strengths and twenty most common weaknesses for each personality type. In fact, it uses the total number of strengths plus the total number of weaknesses in each category to "identify" where you fall on the chart. As we've discussed already, sometimes it is better to "self-assess" based on an overall look at the traits you exhibit and the motivation that you know exists behind each action than to focus too much on a written test. Part of the challenge in this section is to identify any problem areas; then you must decide what to do in response to those observations.

Perhaps the most interesting observation about examining the weaknesses of each color is the notion that each potential weakness is the result of a characteristic that started as a strength being taken too far. Yes, in this context, it is absolutely true that there can be too much of a good thing. Let's look at some examples so you can see what I mean.

Remember those Yellow strengths from Chapter 8 like being able to talk to anyone, being the life of the party, and being spontaneous and fun? What happens when those positive traits are taken too far? You can end up with someone who talks too much, interrupts others, is a poor listener, is distracted, late, or perceived as shallow and insincere. Creativity is a good thing…until the person finds himself or herself drowning in chaos and disorder.

What about the Blues? Order, discipline and a quest for perfection are good…until taken to an extreme and they can become a critical spirit that is harsh or unforgiving, of others or of oneself. An intense need for perfection can paralyze some Blues and keep them from finishing, or sometimes even starting, certain projects. Being good at working independently can also sometimes mean not good at working with others.

Reds have so many natural leadership skills. What happens when that leadership turns into being bossy, rude or arrogant? Reds can be good at seeing the end goal, but need to be careful that they don't "step on people" on the way to the goal. Sometimes they can get so focused on the task(s) at hand, they can forget to focus on people. In an effort to be efficient and successful, they often overlook people's feelings or opinions and become inflexible and controlling.

Greens are so peaceful and easy going…how could those traits possibly become weaknesses? Calmness can become unenthusiastic. Comfort can lead to lack of goals or motivation. Being consistent and steady can turn into a fear of change, indecisiveness, or avoidance of responsibility. In their efforts to get along with everyone, Greens sometimes don't speak up about their own opinions and desires, leaving them to slowly boil beneath the surface...which eventually can lead to an outburst that takes everyone else by surprise.

Okay...now what? So we can agree that every color has some possible challenges in different areas. Now that you are able to identify some of your weaknesses and relate them to personality traits, do you just get a "pass" to explain away and justify bad behavior? WRONG. Becoming aware is only the first step. Once you recognize your weaknesses (challenges, problem areas, blind spots or whatever you want to call them) you must come up with a plan to work on them.

I find the lack of Blue in our home, and business, a great example of this. As you know I am a Red/Yellow. My husband is primarily Green with some Yellow. Neither of us have many Blue traits...nor do ANY of our four children. Our household is definitely on the chaotic side because of the heavy Yellow influence. But rather than saying, "Oh well, that's just the way we are" we have to work on it. We have mailboxes on the wall in the hallway to help us sort mail and school papers. There are cubbies near the front door to house shoes, jackets and backpacks. We have a chore chart to help keep track of whose turn it is for dishes, trash and vacuuming. We don't execute these plans flawlessly, but we do try. Recognizing that some of these things don't come naturally to us, just means that we really have to work at them.

This example also holds true for our business. My husband and I have owned one or more businesses for over twenty years. Even though we know that we are not naturally good with numbers and details, we don't get to hide behind that excuse. We can't tell our employees that we got too distracted by more fun stuff than doing payroll so they'll have to wait until the following week to get their checks. (We wouldn't have employees for long if we did that.) And we certainly can't tell the IRS that we aren't going to do taxes this year because that stuff isn't part of our natural personalities. We have a few options for situations like this. We can either WORK AT becoming good at the things we aren't naturally good at, OR we can find a way to utilize the skills of someone else who is good at them.

In our case, we've decided that most of the "home stuff" we can handle with only a little outside help. We rotate the daily chores, work together to catch up when we get behind, and also have a housecleaner who comes every few weeks to make sure we don't get too far behind. As for the "business stuff," the stakes are higher so we use a payroll service to make sure that our employees all get paid via direct deposit every two weeks. And, we have a CPA who handles our taxes. Recognizing your weaknesses isn't enough. You must own them and come up with a plan to overcome them.

In the next section, we'll look at how the different colors' strengths and weaknesses affect relationships. For now though, focus on your OWN weaknesses and what you can do to work on those areas. I know it's really easy to see the weaknesses that other people need to work on. If you find yourself in that situation, consider buying them copies of this book. (Please don't take it personally if someone gave you the copy you are reading now...it probably wasn't because of this chapter.)

Personal Reflection or Group Discussion

1. What are your weaknesses? Be honest with yourself, but not overly critical.
2. How do those areas that don't come natural for you affect you within your role in your business?
3. How might these areas be affecting your relationship with your team? With your clients?

4. Note: If you are using this for group discussion, please be sensitive. Keep your sharing focused on yourself this time rather than pointing out the flaws or challenges of others.

To Go Deeper - Use the Self-Improvement Tool. The examples given are only a starting point. What is your biggest hurdle that you want to work on in this area? What strategy(ies) will you use to try to work on that issue this week? Write it down. Talk about it with a trusted friend or another member of your team. Ask him to check in with you throughout the week to see how you are doing.

BONUS — SELF-IMPROVEMENT TOOL

Use this simple tool to help you come up with a plan. Think about your own personality color. What negative tendencies do you have? Choose one (maybe two) traits to work on this week. Come up with a strategy to help you improve and PRACTICE your chosen strategy every day for an entire week. I have given you one possible example for each color to help get you started. If it helps you track this journey, write down a short summary of your feelings and observations about this issue at the end of each day. Look back at the end of the week and see how far you have progressed. Repeat again the following week for the same trait, or select another one to work on. Repeat as needed!

Weakness	Strategy to Work On
(Y) Talking more than listening	Stop yourself and only say HALF of what pops into your head
(B) Being overly critical	Practice giving sincere compliments; one to an employee or colleague, and one to yourself… every day.
(R) Focusing on tasks at the expense of the people involved	Build in a "buffer" to your meetings and use that time to try to get to know people. Start with making small talk and gradually go deeper and more personal.

(G) Lack of motivation and/ or laziness	Set a goal and take ONE step closer to it each day. Write it down and do it. Ask someone (preferably a Red or Blue) to keep you accountable each day on your progress.

This week I am working on _____
_____. My plan is to _____
_____
_____.

Today's date: _____

Day 1	
Day 2	
Day 3	
Day 4	
Day 5	
Day 6	
Day 7	

For a full color downloadable PDF of this Bonus page please go to www.VickieMusni.com/SMARTbonuses.

S

M

A

Relationships

T

CHAPTER 11

The World is a Colorful Place

What is your favorite color? Now…imagine that your ENTIRE wardrobe was exclusively that color. Picture every single thing in your home and office that color. The walls…the floor…the furniture… your dishes, flatware, every book on your bookshelf, and every item on your desk. The picture in my mind is not a pretty one. I love the color red. I used to wear a lot of red. I had red sweaters, red dresses, and of course multiple pairs of red heels and boots. Then, I decided to dye my hair red. I love it. This is probably the longest I've kept the same hair color in my entire adult life. But the irony is that I seldom wear red. I did keep the red boots, but all my red tops and dresses have been given away. Now I wear a lot of greens and blues. Why? Because those colors go really well with my red hair and green eyes!

Now, imagine your world with only one color personality. At first it may not seem so bad…*hey, everyone thinks like me*. But after a while you might have a moment when you realize…*everyone thinks like me and that is NOT good! Where are the people who have different ideas? Where are the people who are good at the things that I struggle with?*

Relationships is the perfect section to follow the *Abilities* section because understanding each color's natural abilities and tendencies is the key to understanding how the different personalities interact together. Recognizing that some of my weaknesses are another color's strengths, and vice versa, helps us not only understand but *enjoy* the colorful world we live in. We truly NEED all of the color personalities. At a larger, societal level, we need all types of people... the creative, the deep thinkers, the bold and courageous doers, and the slow and steady, methodical doers. We need them all. At an individual level this is also true.

Think about the relationships you have and have had with people very close to you. My mother and I are a lot alike; she is a Red/Yellow. My dad, however, is a Blue/Green. Even though I didn't understand it the same way that I do now, I observed this dynamic for the 19 years I lived at home, and still see it every time we visit them. My dad was an engineer for General Electric for over 30 years. It was the perfect job for him involving detailed, analytical assignments, that typically only changed every five years or so. My mom was a mostly stay-at-home mom who managed all the activities that my three brothers and I were involved in. For years she juggled baseball, hockey, piano lessons, Girl Scouts, Boy Scouts, choir and more, while teaching classes at church, leading women's groups, tutoring the neighbor's children, and generally taking care of anyone who needed it. My dad was around a lot, but he was fine supporting in the background, driving us to and fro, attending games and performances, and of course paying all the bills for the household, including all of our activities and outings. They always have been, and still are (over 46 years later), good at doing what they each do best naturally, and providing the kind of balance of skills and temperament that the other one needs.

I see similar patterns in my own life, although my husband and I are not quite as balanced as my parents as neither of us possesses many Blue traits, if any. My Red side is very high strung and controlling. Occasionally, those controlling strengths can be a good thing because I manage multiple businesses, lots of volunteer involvement, and like my parents, we also have four children. However, often those traits create an unhealthy, off-balanced, stressful environment. I am continually grateful for the peaceful calmness that my Green husband brings to our household. He may not always respond to things or situations at the pace that my Red wishes he did, but his steady calmness is what our family needs to balance me out. And sometimes my Yellow can help him find his inner Yellow and try something new, meet someone new, or visit someplace new. Is it any wonder that so often opposites attract? There are great benefits when different colors coexist together, each drawing upon his or her own strengths and relying on the other to fill in the gaps where we lack.

My husband and I also run a business together. There are times when it's really good that I am Red. I can see something that needs to be addressed or changed, and do it. I notice an issue with an employee, and I can have the direct conversation that needs to happen. I can juggle the last minute changes in the schedule and make sure that everyone knows where they need to be. There are so many times when I am incredibly thankful that my husband is a Green. Our business needs that balance. I rely on him to quietly take care of certain tasks that he does faithfully. I need him to calm me down when I am upset. Sometimes he will be the one to talk to a client who is upset because he is so much better at keeping his cool than I am. Opposite personalities can bring an important balance.

Think about your relationships at home and at work. What colors do you see?

Personal Reflection or Group Discussion

1. In which areas of your business life can you see different colors balancing each other out?
2. How can you learn from the people who are different from you?
3. How can you balance each other out?

To Go Deeper - Keeping in mind the previous discussions on strengths and weaknesses, what is one example in your business where different personality colors are working well together? Are there things you do in your business to make sure that your team is experiencing the maximum benefit from the synergy that is coming from that pairing?

CHAPTER 12

Clashing Colors

Some colors seem to naturally look great together. Other color combinations seem to clash...until an artist comes along and makes one small change, and voila! A masterpiece! The same can be said for personality colors. Some colors seem to get along really well together most of the time. Other color combinations seem to clash. I want you to become the artist who knows how to make small adjustments to the "shade" of a conversation or relationship and help turn something that was clashing into something beautiful. Understanding the other person's perspective is the key to working through many situations that involve clashing personalities.

Generally speaking, different shades of the same color tend to go well together...both in art and in personalities. Yellows tend to enjoy and have fun with other Yellows. Blues like thinking deeply with other Blues – one at a time, of course. Greens get along with practically everyone, but they can find hanging out with other Greens particularly relaxing. Reds seem to be the most common exception. If both Reds are focused on the same goal, then yes, they can accomplish great things together. But two or more Reds together, is the most likely combination to experience conflict, often as a result of a power struggle. (Think hot pink and bright red...no matter what you do with that, they clash.)

As a kid, I always loved learning about the color wheel and primary, secondary, and tertiary colors. I even took a class called "Color" as an elective when I was in college. I love that colors opposite of each other on the color wheel are called "complementary" colors. But I also remember learning in my art classes that some of the best combinations happen when you start with a complementary color scheme, but tweak one of the colors one spot to either side on the color wheel. Take my love of Red and Green from earlier as an example. Red and Green are complementary colors on the color wheel. (And, they just happen to be opposite personality colors on our chart!) If you have a true red and a true green together in equal proportion, often those colors will clash (or make you look like a Christmas decoration). Shifting the red to orange can soften things and can make the green look better. Once again, this concept seems to hold true in relation to personality colors.

Opposite personalities (Yellows and Blues, Reds and Greens) can also sometimes have a "clashing" effect. Yellows may feel offended by Blues who want to shake hands, when the Yellow is more of a "hugger." Blues can get frustrated with Yellows who are noisy, distracted, or late. Reds and Greens often disagree on what the best "pace" is for working on a project. It is important to understand that most of these clashes are rooted in the specific opposite traits of opposite personalities.

Sometimes simply understanding this is enough to help alleviate tension in a situation. Recognizing that not everyone thinks like you is an important first step. You, the artist who understands personalities, have to be the one to look at a situation *in color*. Is it possible that her different approach to a problem might be a good thing? Could it be that his demeanor is not intended to be malicious or offensive, but he may just have an opposite personality from you? Try to assume the best about the other person. Most of the time, they are approaching the project the way their personality functions best. Give them the benefit of the doubt instead of acting as if they are out to harm you or make things more difficult for you.

In *Personalities for Business*, I shared a story of a position I held where the team of Blue and Red managers gave me a laundry list of my mistakes at my annual review before telling me how impressed they were with my sales numbers and performance. Understanding personalities helped me see this situation for what it was – Reds who were trying to be efficient and Blues who kept detailed lists. Because I could see this situation in color, I was able to realize what was happening, and articulate that my personality needed some praise and validation to balance out the suggestions for improvement.

As in the example above, understanding the colorful dynamics at play in the situation helped me see things differently. But, I also had to speak up. As the one who is reading this book and trying to understand personalities, you need to be the one who takes action or tries to change something. You can't change anyone else's thoughts or actions, but you are in control of yours. If you are wise, you may be able to help bring some more color clarity to the situation.

Now think back to my illustration from the beginning of this chapter with the so-called complementary colors on the color wheel. What would be the personality equivalent of shifting to the next color to create a more harmonious outcome than the two original colors that were opposite on the color wheel? In this case, it simply means trying to shift your "opposite" thinking and actions to be a little closer to the other person's color. Let's break this idea down in more detail.

Look at the chart from Section 1. There is one square in either direction between your primary personality color and the color opposite yours on the chart. And if you have a strong secondary color, that color is closer to the opposite color, right? Colors that are touching on the chart are naturally going to have more overlap in traits. Trying to shift into your secondary color mode will help you shift one color closer to the person you are "clashing" with. Here is a personal example. My Red often conflicts with my husband's Green. Instead of being "all Red" if I can make a conscious choice to lean Yellow, I am one step closer to his Green. The common bond between Yellow and Green is that both of those colors tend to be people oriented. If I can make sure my comments and my tone are sensitive and caring, the chances of decreasing conflict increase greatly.

In the situation where I was working with the Blue/Red team, as someone who is half Yellow, I needed to intentionally try to lean Red. For me, that meant lowering my voice when working in the office, and staying focused on the tasks related to serving our clients. Even though part of my job was building relationships with clients, I needed to find a way to be "social" with them that didn't bother my Blue colleagues.

Think about the people you work with who you seem to clash with the most. How can you "frame" your conflicts in terms of personalities? Perhaps you are a Green trying to please a Red boss. One of your struggles is likely to be working at the pace they do and finishing tasks according to their Red expectations. Whether you try to channel some Yellow energy and make a game of your to-do list to help you work faster, or you look to the Blue side to help you turn off noisy distractions and stay focused, you will be one step closer to Red.

What if you are the Blue trying to work with a Yellow? They seem to get excited about a new idea, but you may not want to back them. You either immediately see all the problems and potential pitfalls, or expect them to lose interest and move onto something else. Whether your hesitation is because of design flaws or your lack of confidence in their leadership style, how can you be expected to be positive when you assume the project is doomed to failure? Your first reaction as a Blue might be to make a list of all the things that could go wrong. Being able to spot potential flaws is not a bad thing, but focusing exclusively on the negative can be. What if you tried to be more Red?

Can you up your energy level and try to find a way to solve those potential issues that you've identified? Or can you look to Greens for examples of ways to be supportive? How can you break this big Yellow idea down into simpler steps to make it easier to approach? Can you find *something* good in there and offer some praise?

You have the knowledge you need to begin to train yourself to approach difficult relationships and situations this way. It isn't always easy, but you can learn how to do it. Now imagine how peaceful and productive your workplace could become if every person on your team knew how to see in color. Together you can create a masterpiece.

Personal Reflection or Group Discussion

1. Is there one color (or one person) that your personality tends to clash with?
2. Think of a specific recent situation. What could you have said or done differently that might have helped smooth things out?
3. Is there something that you could or should do right now that could help mend a clashing business relationship? Do it.

To Go Deeper - Examine any clashing color relationships among your team or between team members and clients. Are there any situations where you could try to intervene as a supervisor or as a peer? How can you use the idea of shifting one color to reduce tension between certain individuals?

BONUS — YOUR FAMILY TREE

The focus of this book is business, but we all also have a personal life. To take a deeper look at your family's personality colors, here are some personal questions for reflection. If you feel comfortable, discuss them with your partner, a parent, a sibling, or even your child(ren) depending on their age.

For Reflection or Discussion

ROOTS - Take a look at your parents and/or those who influenced your early years. (1) What colors were the authority figures in your home? (2) How did those colors interact with yours? Were you more complementary or clashing? (3) How do the color relationships from your childhood affect you as an adult?

TRUNK - If you are married or in a serious long-term relationship, look at your colors and how they interact. (1) Are you and your spouse matching in color? Opposites? Overlapping blends? (2) How do you see your color differences and similarities affecting your home life? (3) How can understanding personality colors help you resolve conflicts sooner?

BRANCHES - Look at your children. (1) What color(s) do you see? (2) What do you notice about the various relationships among those with similar or opposite colors? (3) Are there any patterns from your childhood that you see? What would you like to replicate and what patterns would you like to avoid? (4) How can you use your understanding of personality colors to help you reduce and resolve conflicts? (5) How can you encourage your children to grow in accordance with their unique color and strengths?

For a full color downloadable PDF of this Bonus page please go to www.VickieMusni.com/SMARTbonuses.

S
M
A
R
Teams

CHAPTER 13

What Team? I Work Alone.

It is very likely that many of you reading this book might fall into the category of "solopreneurs" or business owners who don't have any employees. Don't stop reading! Even if you have no intention of ever growing your business in a way that will lead you to hiring a team of employees, there are still principles that apply to you.

Assuming you have been reading the sections in order, by now you should have done some self analysis and have realized that even if you wear many figurative hats in your business, you aren't likely to be equally great in all areas. Each personality comes with its own strengths and weaknesses. In the relationship section we discussed how important it is to have people to help balance out your traits. If you don't have any employees - and don't plan to - who might those other people be?

Basketball legend John Wooden is known for having said, "Whatever you do in life, surround yourself with smart people who'll argue with you." As a Personality Trainer, I would paraphrase this to read something like, "Whatever you do in life, surround yourself with opposite personalities who will help you think critically about situations and decisions." Do you already have people in your life who fit that general description? Do you have a spouse or partner who you can bounce ideas off of or who can help you calm down or re-focus if needed? Do you have an industry colleague or a friend in a similar business who understands the specific challenges that you face? Consider those people part of your "team" even if they aren't on your payroll.

Do you remember the example I shared in Chapter 10 about the lack of "natural" Blue in our company? There are certain tasks that we decide to hire out. Do you have a bookkeeper or accountant? What about a graphic designer? Web designer? Virtual assistant? Business coach? Suppliers or vendors you buy from regularly? Consider some of these people part of your team. How can you utilize their expertise to help you grow, both personally and professionally? How can you intentionally cultivate those relationships?

Are you part of a mastermind or networking group? As a solopreneur, I encourage you to look for other solopreneurs so you can all begin to benefit from having a team of different personalities. Networking with other business owners, even those who may be outside of your industry niche, can still help you feel like you are part of a team or group. There are lessons we can learn from someone else's experience. There are lessons we can learn from someone else's perspective.

Identify any of these people who might make up part of the extended "team" for you and your business. Now think about the individual personalities. Do you see any color patterns? Are there some people who you like and connect with who are the same color(s) as you? Are there others in your circle of influence who have an opposite personality color that complements your personality well? Hang on to those people. Invest in those relationships. Even if you run your business alone, you don't have to be completely alone in your business. Find your team.

Personal Reflection or Group Discussion

1. Make a list of people who are part of your "team" for your business.
2. Identify the color(s) of each person on your list.
3. How do those colors compare to your own? Do you have people who help bring a balanced perspective to the way you do business?

To Go Deeper - Analyze your "team" a little further. Who or what might be missing? Can you identify a friend or colleague who might help fill that gap? What can you do to improve or strengthen or even begin that relationship? Write out a game plan and include specific steps like a mastermind group you'd like to join, a networking group you could be more involved in, or a mentor you'd like to reach out to.

CHAPTER 14

Your Company Color Palette

Team building: the ability to identify and motivate individual employees to form a team that stays together, works together, and achieves together. That is from the description for "team building" at Businessdictionary. com. Part of team building then is learning about the team you have (motivation), and part of it is carefully building onto that team (identify and achieve). Who is "missing" from your current team? Who are you looking for next?

In his book, *Good to Great*, author Jim Collins talks about the importance of "getting the right people on the bus, the wrong people off the bus, and the right people in the right seats."

First, look at your current team. What colors make up your company? If you haven't been doing so as you've been reading, stop now and analyze your current team. If you are part of a relatively small company and know everyone fairly well, you should be able to make an educated guess as to where each team member falls. If you aren't sure, consider having everyone take the 40-question *Wired That Way* assessment and spending some time discussing the results as a team (or with me if you want to schedule customized team training).

Next, analyze your observations. Do you have more of one color than the others? Or is there a fairly even split? Look at primary and secondary types (blends) to get a better feel for the overall color palette of your team. Are there common traits that stand out to you or things that you notice about certain people or departments? How is this color scheme affecting the day to day interactions of the staff?

A few years ago, I was hired to do a training for a group of engineers. They knew that something was "off" in the office and it was impacting communication, productivity, and morale. Before meeting with the group in person, I had them all take the WTW assessment and send me their results. In under a minute, I could identify their biggest challenge. Eleven out of the 14 employees were either a primary or secondary Red. They had one Yellow in the group (who had already requested a transfer) and ZERO Greens among them. They were not only out of balance, but also they were heavy in the personality most likely to clash with others of the same color. Team training can help if you find yourself in a situation like this, but hopefully, through understanding personalities you can continue to build your team in a way that brings harmony to your company color palette.

Sometimes, the challenge lies in the individual job descriptions even more so than how the team interacts together. Remember the story from Chapter 8 about the job I had that I loved some days and hated other days? Once I was able to shift certain responsibilities around, I was happier and more productive at work. When I was able to focus on tasks that were naturally suited to my personality I not only had a better attitude, I was more successful and productive.

Are there changes that you can make internally that could help with this? Do you have one person trying to do both front office tasks (answering phones, greeting customers as they enter) and back office tasks (updating spreadsheets, balancing accounting information)? Someone who is split on the extroverted/introverted spectrum – Yellow/Greens or Red/Blues – may be really happy doing both kinds of tasks. But if you have someone like me who is that Red/Yellow split, the lonely and detailed tasks aren't naturally a good fit. And if you have someone who is a complete introvert – Blue/Green – they may not enjoy having to answer the phone or greet people.

I am not trying to say that no one should ever do a task that they don't enjoy. I am, however, suggesting that you look at your job descriptions in color. Consider what percentage of the tasks line up with the individual's strengths and weaknesses. If it's a small number, they may be just fine. But, if a person hates the majority of their job, that is something you will want to look at.

Once you have identified the color of each team member, look at who they are in relation to not only what they do, but who they interact with. Do you have good color combinations working in close proximity, either literally (shared cubicles, neighboring offices, etc.) or figuratively (on joint projects or assigned to the same departments).

If you are the "boss" – be it owner or manager or some other title – how does YOUR personality color affect how you lead? Are you putting the right people in the right "seats" on your bus? While I love the analogy of the bus, I tend to picture my company as having different colored chairs. Each different color chair represents a position in the company. The skills required for that job, and the person sitting in that chair must match. Additionally, the chair must match the workstation, and fit in well with the overall design of the company's color palette.

Think about each position and the skills required to do that job well. What color personality is going to naturally fit in there? Hiring someone whose natural skills match best with the job description is huge in helping set that employee up for success. Being in the right colored chair will tend to lead to increased productivity, improved morale, higher sense of satisfaction and accomplishment, and often increase longevity with the company…which of course contributes to overall increased productivity, improved morale, and so on.

What color is your company? What color(s) might be missing? Are there people whose job descriptions might need to be adjusted? Or new personalities that you need to look for as you grow?

Personal Reflection or Group Discussion

1. What color(s) is YOUR chair? Is it a good fit for you? Are there any adjustments you can make if things don't match well?
2. What color "chairs" are in your workplace? What color person sits in each of those chairs?
3. If you have a situation where someone is in a seat that is the "wrong" color, what do you think can be done?

To Go Deeper - What new seats might need to be added to your company? What color should each one be? Think about the tasks related to each specific job description, as well as how each new chair could affect your current company color palette. Use these answers as you move forward in recruiting and interviewing candidates for open positions.

CHAPTER 15

What color is Achievement?

Motivation and training are important components in building a team "that stays together, works together, and achieves together." (Remember that definition from the previous chapter?) And of course, like every other aspect of business that we've examined so far, personality colors play a big part in moving a team forward toward achieving the desired goals.

Personalities for Business, has a whole chapter devoted to motivation. Let's review for those who have read it, and summarize for those who have not.

Yellows – need fun, attention, & affection	Reds – efficiency, action, & results
Strategies to Try:	Strategies to Try:
• Give them a special job/role • Make meetings feel like a "gathering" or even a party • Collaborative projects • Opportunities to talk • Channel their enthusiasm but don't squelch it	• Be concise and focused • Discuss things in terms of measurable results • Set goals together • Measure – and announce – personal accomplishments • Allow them some control/autonomy

Greens – need comfort & stability	Blues – need accuracy, order, & facts
Strategies to Try:	Strategies to Try:
• Establish predictable routines • Announce any changes well in advance/avoid big "surprise" announcements • Create a comfortable work environment • Show support and acknowledge their contributions to the team	• Always know your facts • Provide as many details as possible – in writing, or in the form of charts, graphs or tables • Analyze pros & cons • Be creative, thoughtful and organized with your requests, ideas and meetings

Keep these things in mind as you are planning meetings and discussing projects or tasks. Make sure you are looking at goal setting *in color*. First, look at your own personality. Just because you might be the "boss" does not automatically mean you are good at looking ahead and setting weekly, monthly, quarterly or annual goals...or 5 or 10 year goals. But this need to be done; AND you will need to share these goals with your team in a way that motivates ALL of you to stay on track and keeps you working together toward the desired results.

Review the "Abilities" section and think about your own strengths and weaknesses in terms of goal setting. Does planning long-term goals and breaking them down into shorter-term goals and daily tasks come easy to you? Do you need to find a mentor or hire a coach to help you with this? Is there someone on your team who would be great at working on this with you?

Once you have figured out your strategy for this, how will you communicate this vision to your team? Look at the colors of your team. What do they need to best hear you, best see your vision, and understand the direction the team is heading? How can you make it fun and exciting for your Yellows? Can you track progress visually and celebrate smaller goals along the way? Give them something fun to look forward to. Do you have all the details that your Blues need to get on board? Have you done your research? How can you utilize their skills in this area? The graphs may not be as fanciful as if you have a Yellow charting the progress, but with Blues working on this, you will know where you stand, and what still remains to be done.

Reds tend to be naturally good at goal setting and are often self-motivated. Use their energy and skills in this area to help keep others focused on the goal, and don't neglect to thank them for the leadership they provide to the team and acknowledge their progress along the way. Greens sometimes need the most help in the motivation department. Paint the picture for them, helping them see how each goal is important to the company and to them. Make transitions as easy as possible, offering support as they learn new tasks or procedures. Build them up individually and they will become huge assets to you in the building up of your entire team.

As the team works together to reach new heights, training and professional development are likely to come into play. Part of team building is teaching new skills and reinforcing desired behaviors and processes. The reason I've left training and motivation in the same chapter is that the recommended strategies are essentially the same. People are more motivated to do something when the way it's presented is in line with how they think and the things they value. They are also more likely to learn and retain information if you are creating an environment that fits with their color.

Yellows and Greens tend to like group learning. Reds can be okay with group sessions, if they get to be in charge, but Blues usually prefer to do things on their own. Most Yellows are willing to try something, even if they might not be good at it right away, so performance training, role plays and situational learning can be great for them. Like Yellows, Reds are typically quick to volunteer and okay with activities that require them to think on their feet. Generally speaking, Blues are going to want more time to read everything and process the information, before they are willing to try something in front of their peers. Greens also tend to prefer to process information internally before answering questions or giving examples in front of their colleagues.

It is definitely more work for you as a business owner or team leader to create training opportunities that are customized to each team member's preferred learning style. But, if you want "picture perfect" results, make sure you have at least one element in your training geared to each person's personality color.

Personal Reflection or Group Discussion

1. What goals is your team working toward currently? What systems do you already have in place to measure progress and encourage involvement?
2. How can you use your personality's natural strengths to help you set goals for yourself and your team? Are you good at making them fun? Or detailed? Do your strengths lie in seeing where you want to be and creating a direct path to get there? Or are you good at finding simple solutions to one obstacle at a time?
3. How can you help motivate others on your team to work together to achieve goals as a team? Think specifically about what each color needs most.

To Go Deeper - For more ideas on training in color, go back and look at the motivational summary chart at the beginning of this chapter. How can those lists help you make some small changes in your current continuing education that could yield some big results for your team?

BONUS – IDEAS FOR A
COLORFUL TEAM RETREAT

Create a retreat that includes a mix of evaluation and planning with fun and relaxation. If you have a committee, try to make sure that each personality color is on your committee.

Consider some of these thoughts as you plan:

How can all personalities enjoy the game(s) that you are planning? Is there a way for it to be social without making introverts uncomfortable? Is it fun with a purpose so Reds don't see it as a waste of time? Can there be a competitive element without the "losers" feeling punished?

Evaluation of the previous year and goal setting for the next period are both important. How can you go over details with the team in a way that is complete, but not overwhelming? How can you make facts and figures fun?

How can you create opportunities for people to choose certain tasks they wish to be involved in? Can some activities be optional? Remember that while some need a little downtime, others want to be always going, always working on something. How can you meet both unique needs?

Naturally good at: FUN **Put them in charge of:** games, decorations, optional/extra activities **Be sure to ask them:** what they think about policies and procedures. Find out what is working for them and what is not; they may be hesitant to share details about challenges.	**Naturally good at:** PLANNING **Put them in charge of:** keeping the group on time, vision-casting and goal setting **Be sure to ask them:** what helps them relax; this will help them realize that this part of the retreat is important too. Who do they think should lead certain activities or discussions? Help them delegate and let others lead.
Naturally good at: COMFORT **Put them in charge of:** the environment (layout or room, seating), supporting roles, snacks and breaks **Be sure to ask them:** what is important to them. Just because Greens may be slower to speak up does not mean that they don't have opinions and ideas. Ask questions and wait patiently for their answers.	**Naturally good at:** DETAILS **Put them in charge of:** reports and projections, taking notes **Be sure to ask them:** what sounds fun to them; their ideas on fun might be different. Ask them to identify what they see that is working well; some Blues have a harder time articulating positives.

For a full color downloadable PDF of this Bonus page please go to www.VickieMusni.com/SMARTbonuses.

SECTION 7

CHAPTER 16

Seeing in Color

Sales, Marketing, Abilities, Relationships, Team-building. You've been SMART to read each section and I thank you for making it this far with me. I hope that along the way you paused to examine each area and took time to really see yourself, and those around you, in color. If you did just read straight through, I urge you to go back and reflect on the questions in each section. Do some of the activities. Work through the bonus material.

My hope is that rather than closing the book and thinking to yourself, "Check. What's next on my list?" or "Yay me, I finished a book!" that it will truly have a lasting impact on you and those around you.

I remember watching the *Wizard of Oz* as a kid. Every year (yes, it only came on television once a year so we had to wait to watch it) I would look forward to that moment when Dorothy would step out of her tossed-around house and into Munchkinland where everything she saw was suddenly in full color. It was magical. She saw things differently. She saw people from her "old life" in a completely new way, and learned what it was that each person needed most. I wish that kind of magic on you as you begin to see yourself, your team, your clients, and other people that you meet in full color.

May the imagery and examples shared in this book be only a beginning for you. May the "language" of color become a part of your company culture and the way you communicate internally. May it increase your understanding, help you improve your communication, and help you connect with people more deeply as you continue to grow your business.

I invite you to share your stories with me as you begin to see in color. You are welcome to contact my Facebook page or visit VickieMusni. com for more information and resources. Please consider sharing a review on Amazon or Facebook. Most importantly, don't let the message of seeing in color go dark. Keep the SMART acronym where you can see it – and each area of business it represents – in full color.

Personal Reflection or Group Discussion

1. How comfortable do you feel now with the concept of "seeing in color" as outlined in this book?
2. Which area (Sales, Marketing, Abilities, Relationships or Team-building) has you the most excited now that you have finished reading?
3. What small change do you want to implement today that will help you create a company culture of personality colors? This week? This month? This year?

To Go Deeper - Who else inside your company or within your sphere of influence could benefit from seeing each area of business through the lens of color? How can you use what you have learned to help others see in color? Find someone else to help keep you accountable for personal growth in this area...someone who will check in with you periodically to review the discussion questions with you or help you work through the bonus material. Learning to change the way you see takes time and practice!

Meet Vickie

Certified Personality Trainer Vickie Musni is an International Speaker, Business Coach and Trainer. As a former high school teacher and an experienced business owner, she takes her gift of teaching to new audiences in the form of keynotes, seminars, and interactive workshops.

She is the author of *Personalities for Business* and co-author of *Personalities for Educators* and *Creating Connections: 31 Days to Building Stronger and Deeper Relationships.* Vickie is also the co-host of the weekly video podcast *Creating Connections for Event Pros,* and owns an entertainment company in Reno, Nevada where she lives with her husband and 4 school-aged children.

www.VickieMusni.com   f in   775-772-9188

Book Vickie

"I have seen Vickie speak multiple times and I have taken her Power of Personalities workshop. I have taken away from her workshop and presentations ideas and methodology that has helped my business, especially when it comes to sales and interpersonal communication. I have successfully learned how to identify the differing personalities and how to approach them."   - Rob Ferre, Salt Lake City, Utah

"Booking Vickie to train my team was one of the BEST business and personal decisions I ever made. Informative, extremely fun and interesting throughout, Vickie identifies the missing link most of us suffer with in our business and personal relationships. She helps you understand it, fix it, and it becomes woven into your everyday life." - Aldo Ryan, New York City

www.VickieMusni.com   f in   775-772-9188

Personalities for Business: *The Busy Business Owner's Guide to Increasing Sales & Improving Business Relationships* Vickie's original book on personality colors and how to begin to apply personalities to the way you approach sales, networking, and how you run your office.

Creating Connections: *31 Days to Building Stronger & Deeper Relationships* Join Vickie and Co-Author Mitch Taylor on a month long journey of daily insights and action challenges. Enjoy daily emails as you read by signing up for the 31 Day Challenge at CreatingConnections.BIZ

Personalities for Educators: *The Busy Teacher's Guide to Increasing Participation & Improving Classroom Relationships* Vickie teams up with her brother, Co-Author Kevin Burrill, to bring the colorful world of personalities into a classroom near you. This is the perfect tool for teachers, parents, support staff and administrators alike.

Vickie Musni & Kevin Burrill